THE FREEDOM TRAIL

Joanne Mattern

Rourke
Educational Media

rourkeeducationalmedia.com

Before Reading:

Building Academic Vocabulary and Background Knowledge

Before reading a book, it is important to tap into what your child or students already know about the topic. This will help them develop their vocabulary, increase their reading comprehension, and make connections across the curriculum.

1. Look at the cover of the book. What will this book be about?
2. What do you already know about the topic?
3. Let's study the Table of Contents. What will you learn about in the book's chapters?
4. What would you like to learn about this topic? Do you think you might learn about it from this book? Why or why not?
5. Use a reading journal to write about your knowledge of this topic. Record what you already know about the topic and what you hope to learn about the topic.
6. Read the book.
7. In your reading journal, record what you learned about the topic and your response to the book.
8. After reading the book complete the activities below.

Content Area Vocabulary

Read the list. What do these words mean?

abolitionist
apprentice
cemeteries
citizens
designed
dome
monument
mosaic
Puritans
rebellion
sexton
sites
tourists

After Reading:

Comprehension and Extension Activity

After reading the book, work on the following questions with your child or students in order to check their level of reading comprehension and content mastery.

1. Do you have to follow the Freedom Trail in a particular order? Explain. (Asking Questions)
2. What was the significance of the Boston Massacre? (Summarize)
3. Have you visited a historical site? Share that experience with us. (Text to self connection)
4. What is the importance of preserving history like that found on the Freedom Trail? (Asking Questions)
5. Why is it called the Freedom Trail? (Inferring)

Extension Activity

Take a trip back in time! Research the events that led to the Boston Massacre. Did you find any conflicting information during your search? Who was to blame for the events that happened? Now write a letter to the editor as a witness of the Boston Massacre. You will tell your side of the story and who you feel is to blame for the events and why. Share your letter with your parents, teacher, or classmates.

TABLE OF CONTENTS

Chapter 1

CREATING THE FREEDOM TRAIL!

Boston, Massachusetts is a city filled with history. The city was founded in 1630, when Massachusetts was a British colony. Boston became one of the centers of action during the 1770s, as the colonists struggled to become an independent nation. In the days leading up to the American Revolution, many people gathered in Boston to plan and fight for America's freedom. Later, during the Revolution, many places in Boston became **sites** of important events that helped create a new nation.

Millions of people visit Boston every year to see the famous places where history happened hundreds of years ago. Although other cities have historical sites, Boston has organized a special way to see its famous places. In Boston, you can see most of the famous sites by walking a special path called the Freedom Trail.

William Schofield worked for a Boston newspaper called the *Herald Traveler*. Schofield knew that many people came to Boston to see the city's historic sites, but he also knew there was no organized plan that linked the sites together.

The Old North Church

In 1775 the Old North Church hung lanterns to signal Paul Revere's famous "midnight ride" to tell the colonists the British were coming. The Old North Church played an important role in the American Revolution and is one of the most popular stops on the Freedom Trail.

On March 8, 1951, Schofield wrote a column in the *Herald Traveler*. In it, he described his idea to link Boston's important places. Schofield wrote, "All I'm suggesting is that we mark out a 'Puritan Path' or 'Liberty Loop' or 'Freedom Way' or whatever you want to call it, so [visitors and locals will] know where to start and what course to follow.... You could do the trick on a budget of just a few dollars and a bucket of paint. Not only would it add to the personality of the city, but also it would please the **tourists**."

In his column, Schofield also included a rough idea of the sites his path would include. Over the next two weeks, he kept on writing about his idea and even added a few more sites to his list. Many people in Boston liked Schofield's idea. One of them was Mayor John B. Hynes. On March 31, Hynes announced that the city would go ahead with the plan to create a "Freedom Trail." The new Trail was ready to go by June.

Mayor John B. Hynes
(1897–1970)

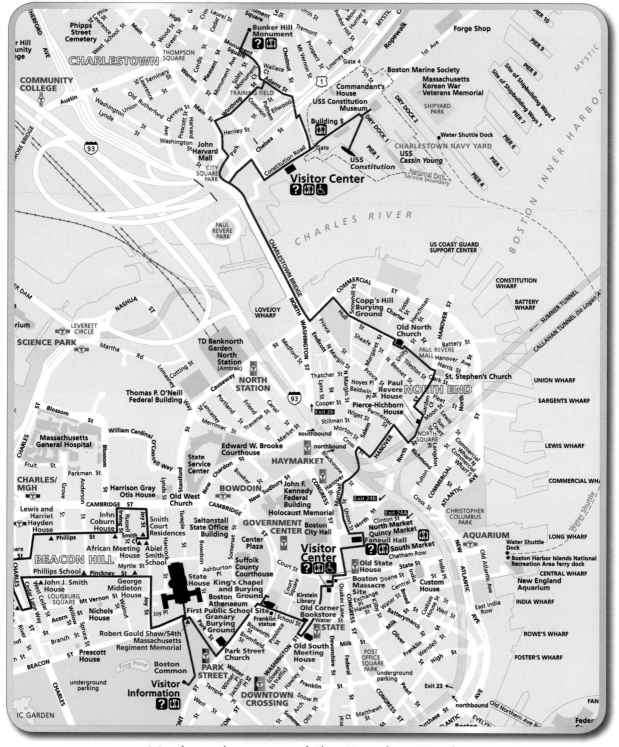

Modern day map of the Freedom Trail.

Over the years, many people have walked the Freedom Trail. During the late 1950s and early 1960s, a local businessman named Dick Berenson made the Trail even better. It was his idea to add a red line to the streets along the Trail. Tourists could follow that line from one site to another. Then, in 1966, the first Freedom Trail Information Center opened at Boston Common, which is the first stop on the Trail. The Information Center provided free maps to visitors. In 1974 the National Park Service created the Boston National Historical Park, which includes eight of the Trail's sixteen sites. Together, these organizations and the city care for the Trail.

Freedom Trail Sites

The sixteen stops on the Freedom Trail include:

1. Boston Common
2. Massachusetts State House
3. Park Street Church
4. Old Granary Burying Ground
5. King's Chapel and Burying Ground
6. First Public School
7. Old Corner Bookstore Building
8. Old South Meeting House
9. Old State House
10. Boston Massacre Site
11. Faneuil Hall
12. Paul Revere House
13. Old North Church
14. Copp's Hill Burying Ground
15. *U.S.S. Constitution*
16. Bunker Hill Monument

Chapter 2

BOSTON COMMON AND THE STATE HOUSE

The first stop on the Freedom Trail is Boston Common. British soldiers camped here when they occupied the city from 1775 to 1776. Boston Common has seen many different uses over its long history. For many years, it was the site of public meetings and was the center of Boston's public life. Until 1817 public hangings took place on the Common. The Common was also used as a place to graze cattle until 1830.

Today Boston Common is a beautiful park that covers almost 50 acres (20 hectares). It is the oldest park in the United States.

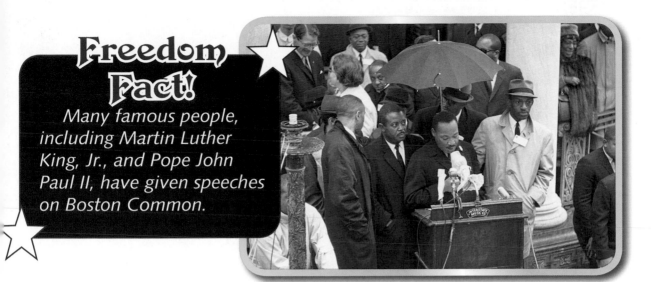

Boston Common is also part of the Emerald Necklace. The Necklace is a system of parks that winds through many of Boston's neighborhoods.

Freedom Trail Site #1 - Boston Common

The next stop on the Trail is the Massachusetts State House, which is right across the street from Boston Common, on top of Beacon Hill. The State House was **designed** by Charles Bullfinch in 1798 and served as the center of the new state's government. It is still the seat of Massachusetts' government today.

Charles Bullfinch (1763–1844)

The State House has several unusual features. The **dome** was originally made out of wood, but now it is covered with a layer of gold. The gold not only looks nice, but it also prevents water from leaking into the building.

Another odd feature is a wooden codfish that hangs in the room where the Massachusetts' House of Representatives meets. This wooden carving is called the Sacred Cod. It is a symbol of the fishing industry in Massachusetts. And since logging was also important in Massachusetts during the 1700s, a wooden pinecone sits on top of the State House's golden dome.

The Sacred Cod, given to the House in 1784 by a Boston merchant, Jonathan Rowe.

Freedom Trail Site #2 -
Massachusetts State House

The Black Heritage Trail

The Freedom Trail is not the only historic walking trail in Boston. As visitors walk toward the Massachusetts State House, they pass the Robert Gould Shaw Memorial. This is the first stop on the Black Heritage Trail, which links sites connected with African-American history in Boston. This trail includes monuments, homes, schools, and meeting places.

Robert Gould Shaw Memorial

Chapter 3

CHURCHES, BURYING GROUNDS, AND MORE

The next part of the Freedom Trail includes many churches and graveyards. Tourists can visit the final resting places of many of Boston's most famous **citizens** along this part of the Trail.

Park Street Church became famous after the Revolution. In fact, it wasn't built until 1809. Its 217 foot (66.1 meter) steeple was so tall that it was the first thing travelers saw when they entered Boston.

Freedom Trail Site #3 - Park Street Church

*William Lloyd Garrison, an **abolitionist**, gave a speech on July 4, 1829 at this church. In his speech, he said that slavery was evil and should be done away with.*

The Old Granary Burying Ground got its name because grain was stored next door where Park Street Church now stands. Started in 1660, the grounds are one of Boston's oldest **cemeteries**. Samuel Adams, John Hancock, and Robert Treat Paine, who all signed the Declaration of

Freedom Trail Site #4 - Old Granary Burying Ground

Independence, are buried here. The burying ground also includes the graves of Paul Revere and the victims of the Boston Massacre.

Continue along the Freedom Trail and you will come to the oldest cemetery in Boston. King's Chapel and Burying Ground was the only cemetery in Boston for thirty years, and it contains the graves of several figures who made history. Probably the most famous is John Winthrop, who was the first governor of the Massachusetts Bay Colony.

Freedom Trail Site #5 - King's Chapel and Burying Ground

Freedom Fact!

King James II of England (1633-1701) ordered King's Chapel to be built so the Church of England would have a church in Boston.

In 1635 the **Puritans** started the first public school in America. Called the Boston Latin School, it began in the home of a teacher named Philemon Pormont. Later the school moved to the site on School Street. Although the building is no longer there, a **mosaic** on the sidewalk marks the spot. Benjamin Franklin attended classes here for a short time. Samuel Adams and John Hancock were also students at Boston Latin School.

Freedom Trail Site #6 - First Public School

Freedom Fact!

The Boston Latin School only admitted boys for more than 300 years. Girls couldn't attend the school until 1972!

Visitors to the site of Boston's first public school pass a statue of Benjamin Franklin (1706–1790), who was one of its students.

The Old Corner Bookstore Building was built in 1712 and was originally an apothecary shop, or drugstore. Many of America's most famous works were published here, including *The Scarlet Letter* by Nathanial Hawthorne and *Walden* by Henry David Thoreau. The Old Corner Bookstore is one of the oldest buildings in Boston.

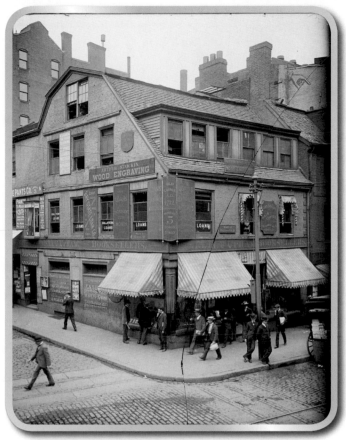

Freedom Trail Site #7 - The Old Corner Bookstore

*Nathanial Hawthorne
(1804–1864)*

*Henry David Thoreau
(1817–1862)*

Chapter 4

MEETING HOUSES AND HOMES

The Freedom Trail is not just cemeteries and government buildings. Several sites were important meeting places, homes, or churches during Revolutionary times.

Few buildings in Boston are as important as the Old South Meeting House. Originally built in 1729, this building became the center of the **rebellion** against British rule. Colonists gathered here to protest the way England treated them. On December 16, 1773, the crowd at the meeting house traveled to the harbor,

"Americans throwing Cargoes of the Tea Ships into the River, at Boston" W.D. Cooper 1789.

where they boarded a British ship and started what became known as the Boston Tea Party.

Freedom Fact! ⭐

The Old South Meeting House was almost torn down in 1876. The people of Boston fought to save the building. Today it is a museum that celebrates Boston's history and free speech.

Freedom Trail Site #8 – Old South Meeting House

Although the Boston Tea Party became famous as a rebellious act by American colonists, it made the rulers in England even angrier at the colonists.

The Old State House was built in 1713 and was the seat of England's colonial government. After the Revolution, the new nation used the building as the Massachusetts State House until 1798. Today the Old State House is a museum all about Boston history.

Freedom Trail Site #9 - The Old State House

FROM THE OLD STATE HOUSE, JULY 18, 1776

Freedom Fact!

On July 18, 1776, Boston's citizens gathered outside the Old State House to hear the Declaration of Independence read from the building's balcony.

The site of the Boston Massacre is in front of the Old State House and is marked by a circle of cobblestones. On March 5, 1770, a street fight began between an **apprentice** and a British soldier. When more soldiers arrived, an angry crowd threw rocks and

Freedom Trail Site #10 - Boston Massacre Site

snowballs at them. The soldiers fired on the crowd, killing five colonists. This event helped lead to the American Revolution.

Faneuil Hall is also called the Cradle of Liberty. The first floor of the hall was a marketplace where people bought and sold goods. Upstairs, however, was a place where colonists met to discuss American independence. One of Faneuil Hall's most famous speakers was Samuel Adams.

Freedom Trail Site #11 - Faneuil Hall

The Paul Revere House is the oldest house in Boston, built around 1680. In 1770 Paul Revere and his family moved into the building and lived there until 1800.

In April 1775 Paul Revere knew that the British were going to attack the area around Boston. The question was, would they come by land or by sea?

Paul Revere (1735–1818). Paul Revere was one of the most important figures of the American Revolution. He was a silversmith and an important citizen in Boston.

Freedom Fact!

During the 1800s, the Paul Revere House was the home of hundreds of Irish, Italian, and Jewish immigrants. The house did not become a museum until 1908.

Freedom Trail Site #12 - Paul Revere House

Revere arranged for Robert Newman, the **sexton** of Old North Church, to signal him with lanterns. One lantern meant the British were coming by land. Two lanterns meant the British were coming by sea. On the night of April 18, Revere got the signal he was waiting for and set out on his "midnight ride" to warn the people of Lexington that the British were arriving by sea.

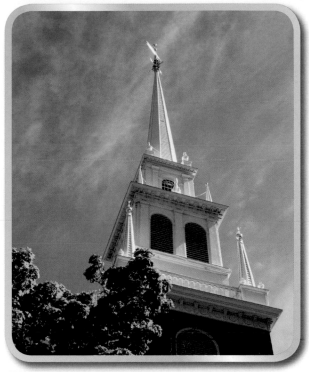

Freedom Trail Site #13 - Old North Church

Freedom Trail Site #14 - Copp's Hill Burying Ground

Copp's Hill Burying Ground is Boston's second oldest cemetery. Founded in 1659, it holds the graves of thousands of Boston's merchants and craftspeople. Robert Newman, the sexton of the Old North Church, is also buried here. Many African-American residents are buried here as well.

Chapter 5

A SHIP AND A MONUMENT

The final two stops on the Freedom Trail are different from the meeting houses, burying grounds, and churches found earlier on the Trail. For this part of the journey, tourists visit a famous ship and the site of an important battle.

The Freedom Trail crosses the Charlestown Bridge into the Navy Yard. The Charlestown Navy Yard was one of the first shipyards in America. The U.S. Navy's oldest warship, the *U.S.S. Constitution*, was built here in 1797. The ship was involved in 42 battles during its long career. One of those battles occurred during the War of 1812, when it received the nickname "Old Ironsides" because British cannonballs bounced off its sides. The *U.S.S. Constitution* was retired in 1881 but still serves as a floating museum.

The U.S.S. Constitution *and* H.M.S. Java *in 1812.*

The U.S.S. Constitution *is the most famous ship in American history. No other ship was undefeated in as many battles.*

Freedom Trail Site #15 - U.S.S. Constitution

Bunker Hill **Monument** honors the first major battle of the American Revolution, which was fought on June 17, 1775. The battle was actually fought on the nearby and smaller Breed's Hill. The poorly trained American Army held off two attacks by the British Army but was finally forced to retreat. Almost half of the British soldiers were killed or injured. The bravery of the American soldiers inspired them to keep fighting the war, even though they lost this battle. Nine months later, George Washington won control of the hill.

"Battle of Bunker Hill" painting by E. Percy Moran. 1862–1935.

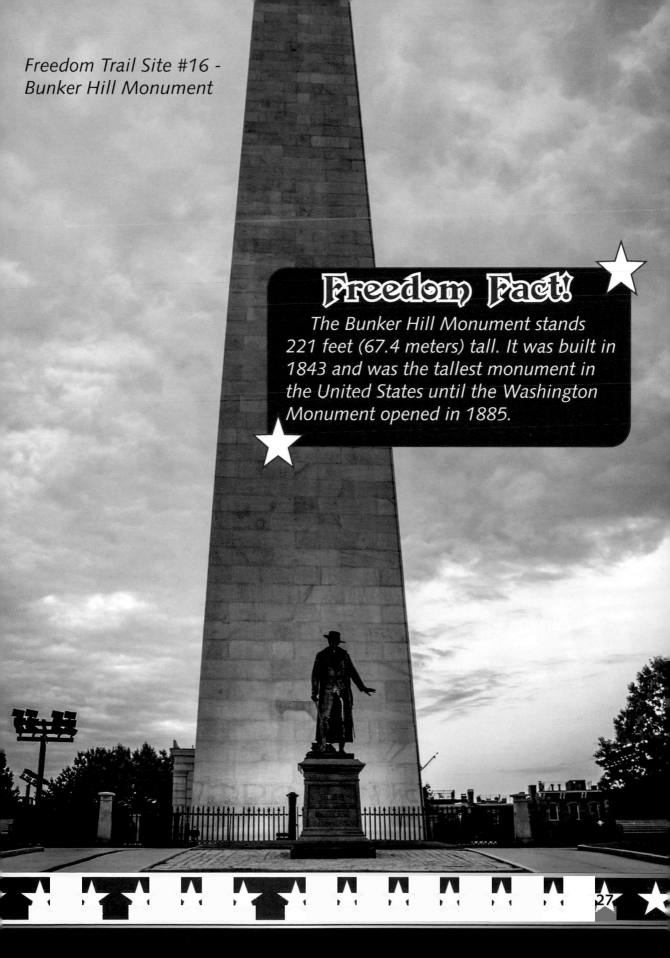

Freedom Fact!

The Bunker Hill Monument stands 221 feet (67.4 meters) tall. It was built in 1843 and was the tallest monument in the United States until the Washington Monument opened in 1885.

Visitors who walk the Freedom Trail cover a lot more ground than the simple two and a half miles (four kilometers) of the route. They take a walk back more than 200 years to retrace the steps of the men and women who fought to create the United States.

Massachusetts State House

TIMELINE

March 8
1951 ——William Schofield writes a newspaper column suggesting a trail to link Boston's historical sites.

March 31
1951 ——Mayor John B. Hynes announces Boston will create a "Freedom Trail."

June
1951 ——The Freedom Trail opens.

Late 1950s-
Early 1960s
——Dick Berenson adds a red line to mark the Freedom Trail.

1966 ——The first Freedom Trail Information Center opens on Boston Common.

1974 ——The National Park Service creates the Boston National Historical Park, which includes eight of the Trail's sixteen sites.

June
2014 ——Boston replaces the Freedom Trail's red paint with a special red, white, and blue plastic strip designed to last for years.

GLOSSARY

abolitionist (ab-uh-LISH-uh-nists): a person who worked to get rid of slavery before the Civil War

apprentice (uh-PREN-tiss): someone who learns a trade or craft by working with a skilled person

cemeteries (SEM-uh-ter-eez): places where dead people are buried

citizens (SIT-ih-zuhnz): people who live in a city or country

designed (dih-ZINED): drew something to be built

dome (DOHM): a roof shaped like half of a sphere

monument (MON-yuh-muhnt): a statue, building, or other structure that reminds people of an event or person

mosaic (moh-ZAY-ik): a picture made up of small pieces of colored stone, tile, or glass

Puritans (PYOOR-uh-tunz): a group of Protestants who left England for America and sought simple church services

rebellion (rih-BEL-yuhn): armed fight against a government

sexton (SEX-tuhn): a person who takes care of a church

sites (SITES): places where something happened

tourists (TOOR-ists): people who travel to visit places for pleasure

INDEX

SHOW WHAT YOU KNOW

1. How many stops are there on the Freedom Trail?

2. Why was the Freedom Trail created?

3. How many people visit the Freedom Trail each year?

4. What is Paul Revere most famous for?

5. How did the Old Granary Burying Ground get its name?

WEBSITES TO VISIT

www.cityofboston.gov/freedomtrail/default.asp

www.aviewoncities.com/boston/freedomtrail.htm

www.thefreedomtrail.org

ABOUT THE AUTHOR

Joanne Mattern has written hundreds of books for children. Her favorite subjects are history, nature, sports, and biographies. She enjoys traveling around the United States and visiting new places. Joanne grew up on the banks of the Hudson River and still lives in the area with her husband, four children, and numerous pets.

Meet The Author!
www.meetREMauthors.com

PHOTO CREDITS: Cover © Robert Morton, Terraxplorer, bwzenith; Title Page © Visions of America, LLC; Page Topper © Todd Arena; page 5 © Library of Congress, Visions of America, LLC; page 6 © Boston Public Library; page 7 © National Park Service; page 8 © Chee-Onm Leong; page 9 © Terraxplorer; page 11 © AP Images, Songquan Deng; page 12 © Allyn Cox, Eric Haynes (Governor's Office), page 13 © WANGKUN JIA, National Gallery of Art; page 14 © Mary Lane; page 15 © River North Photography, Alexius Horatius; page 16 © American Spirit, Daderot; page 17 © Detroit Publishing Company, Library of Congress (Brady-Handy Collection), E.S. Dunshee; page 18 © Library of Congress; page 19 © Detroit Publishing Company (Yale University), Sanual Borges Photography; page 20 © Boston Public Library; page 21 © Mbastos, Mary Lande; page 22 © John Singleton Copley, American Spirit; page 23 © vavalapenler, Henryk Sadura; page 25 © Library of Congress (Detroit Publishing Company), Jeffrey M. Frank; page 26 © Library of Congress (Percy Moran); page 27 © Marcio Joes Bastos Silva; page 28 © Chee-Onm Leong

Edited by: Luana Mitten
Cover and interior design by: Renee Brady

Library of Congress PCN Data

The Freedom Trail / Joanne Mattern
 (Symbols of Freedom)
  ISBN 978-1-63430-045-2 (hard cover)
  ISBN 978-1-63430-075-9 (soft cover)
  ISBN 978-1-63430-104-6 (e-Book)
Library of Congress Control Number: 2014953362

Printed in the United States of America, North Mankato, Minnesota

Also Available as: